DO TURTLES REALLY
BREATHE OUT OF

THEIR **BUMS?**

DR DINO

DO TURTLES REALLY BREATHE OUT OF THEIR BUMS?

DINO

Published by Dino Books,
an imprint of John Blake Publishing Ltd,
3 Bramber Court, 2 Bramber Road,
London W14 9PB, England

www.johnblakepublishing.co.uk

www.facebook.com/Johnblakepub 🟦
twitter.com/johnblakepub 🟦

First published in paperback in 2014

ISBN: 978-1-78219-774-4

British Library Cataloguing-in-Publication Data:

A catalogue record for this book is available from the British Library.

Design by www.envydesign.co.uk

Printed in Great Britain by CPI Group (UK) Ltd

1 3 5 7 9 10 8 6 4 2

Papers used by John Blake Publishing are natural, recyclable products made
from wood grown in sustainable forests. The manufacturing processes
conform to the environmental regulations of the country of origin.

Every attempt has been made to contact the relevant copyright-holders,
but some were unobtainable. We would be grateful if the
appropriate people could contact us.

Introduction

Biology teachers tell kids that they are teaching them about animals. They will tell you about habitats, animal kingdoms, species and, if you've got a truly horrible teacher, even the *Linnaean Classification System*. What they don't tell you is that you aren't learning anything about animals at all. Really, you are being taught how some old blokes decided animals should be 'classified' and 'organised'. Even when they teach you about food chains, they just teach you the boring, obvious stuff, like cows eat grass, and then humans eat cows.

But what about the things you really want and need to know about food chains? Like how the Matamata turtle literally hoovers fish up and into its mouth, or how the electric eel stuns its prey with a huge electric shock, or how the archer fish shoots water at insects to topple them into the water before gobbling them up.

Animals have been around for years and years, way back before humans first evolved – way back, in fact, before my first family, the dinosaurs, ruled the Earth hundreds of millions of years ago. Since then, animals have developed in so many fantastic ways, from animals like chameleons that try to camouflage themselves to hide from hunters in the jungle, to fish in the deep sea that light up all by themselves to help them see. From octopi that have been known to sacrifice one of their wriggling arms to distract a hunter when under attack, to lizards that will drop their tail off if a predator has hold off it. From massive prehistoric 'terror birds' that grew to 3 metres tall and hunted horses, to the hummingbird that is a mere 10 centimetres or so in size but can fly at around 35 miles per hour, there are so many interesting, weird, mind-boggling, incredible facts to learn about the animal world that you just won't learn in the classroom. (And if you do, you have a great teacher. Tell them to send me a letter – I'm always looking for more Assistant Learnatours here.)

So come with me and enter my learnatorium, where you can find out about everything you would never know about slithering snakes, charming chickens, lithe lions and manky monkeys.

Dr Dino

A Little Bit of History First

For years and years, and years and years, and then even more years, the Earth was just a rock floating around in space. Very slowly, over billions more years, life developed – from tiny single-celled organisms to slightly less tiny fish-like things living in the sea. Finally, about 450 million years ago, came an important moment in the history of our planet. A bold fish took a deep breath and flopped out of the sea, becoming the first animal to live

Don't bother, there's nothing here.

permanently on land and beginning the next step along the evolutionary process. Life on Earth would never be the same again.

Now there are estimated to be at least 7.7 million different species of animals around us and this book is all about them (and us).

Kings of the Jungle

Lions are one of the most powerful animals on the planet, and are often called the kings of the animal world. But they can be cut down to size by a pretty small, but spiky, foe – a porcupine. When a lion bends in to take a sniff of this tasty morsel it normally ends up with a sharp reminder to stay away next time... a quill stuck in the jaw. And what's worse, a lion's claws are great for mauling but not very good at gripping, so the wounded big cat will often be stuck with a thorn in its side, or jaw, for life.

Lions are even lazier than your average teenager. They laze around for about twenty hours every day and only hunt for a maximum of four hours, and normally not even that.

The roar of a lion can be heard up to five miles away. To give you an idea of how loud they are, they make more noise than a jackhammer digging up the pavement.

Lions might be the largest of the big cats but they're no match for a cheetah in a race. Cheetahs are the only big cats that don't have retractable claws (retractable claws are claws that can be drawn back into the paw when they aren't needed), which means they can't climb trees, but they can run at a nifty 75 miles per hour – almost three times quicker than Usain Bolt! This makes them the fastest animal on land.

One cat that can climb is the jaguar. In fact these muscular predators can carry twice their body weight up a tree with ease and when they've had their fill they will leave their prey up the nearest tree so that they can come back for seconds later.

If cheetahs would win the 100-metre sprint in the animalympics, then snow leopards would have a good

chance at the long jump. Their hind legs are so strong
that they can jump fifteen metres in one go.

When Cats Attack

Normally, humans aren't on any animals' food chain. That's probably because you aren't tasty enough – I know I prefer a good bit of steak (well, a whole cow if I'm honest) to a human. But sometimes, because of old age or starvation, cats will go after humans and become man-eaters...

The Champawat tigress was the most prolific serial killer of all time... in the animal world. One day, she was out hunting when another hunter, a human, went after her and shot her. She survived but was injured and couldn't hunt her normal prey, so she went after a much easier target... humans. In all she killed 436 people, and the men of the local villages were too scared to go anywhere. The Nepalese government even sent in the army to deal with her, but she was too tricky and escaped. In the end, one brave hunter, a man called Jim Corbett, followed a trail of blood and guts to the wild animal's lair and managed to shoot her dead. Corbett became a hero and went on to have a successful career tracking down a large number of these man-eaters. He even killed the second most prolific animal serial killer – the Leopard of Panar.

You could be forgiven for thinking that big cats are only found in Africa, but in fact they exist all over the world – even in Britain. Although they aren't native animals, collectors bring them over and sometimes they escape. Nobody knows how many there are, but there are hundreds of sightings every year, normally from people who think they see pumas and lynxes. So next time you're out for a walk in the woods, keep an eye out!

Who Likes the Zoo?

The oldest zoo still around today is the Tiergarten zoo at Schonbrunn Palace in Vienna which had 13 animal enclosures when it was opened in 1752. However, there were actually plenty of zoos around before then... they just weren't called zoos (that's the kind of boring word-trickery teachers love to catch you out on). They used to be called menageries and would normally be made up of animals collected by royalty.

The oldest known menagerie was put together around 5,500 years ago in Ancient Egypt. It probably included hippos, elephants and baboons for people to come and stare at.

The Tower of London is famous for holding some of the most important prisoners in Britain – but that wasn't all it had behind bars. For centuries, from about the year 1200, it held London's royal menagerie, and whenever

foreign kings couldn't think of a good gift to give the King (or Queen) of England, they would check to see what they didn't have in the menagerie and give them that. The Tower held everything from lions and leopards to giraffes and monkeys. No wonder escaping was so hard for the prisoners there – even if you dodged the guards you had to get past the hungry lions too!

The Beijing Zoo is one of the biggest and best in the world, and is home to more than 14,500 animals, including its famous giant pandas. Not all zoos in China are quite as good though... One in Henan Province was found to have fake animals on display, including a dog pretending to be a lion and rats posing as snakes!

Out in the wild it's a dog-eat-dog, bird-eat-worm, lion-eat-gazelle, dinosaur-eat-everything-else world. But when animals who would normally be enemies grow up together, it can have unusual results. A bear called Baloo, a lion called Leo and a tiger called Shere Khan were rescued together from a home when they were cubs and became best friends. They all live together in Georgia, USA and play, sleep and eat together without any problems at all!

DO TURTLES REALLY BREATHE OUT OF THEIR BUMS?

Deserted

Deserts are the driest places on Earth – some areas haven't seen rain for more than 500 years, but that doesn't stop some pretty hardy animals from surviving where humans wouldn't be able to last a day.

If you want to impress your friends then you should know that an animal that lives in the desert is called a xerocole. Generally they prefer to only come out at night when it's cooler and many of them are able to estivate – that's the opposite of hibernate by the way – shutting down their bodies for large periods of time over the summer.

Dr Dino's Did You Know?

The camel is the most famous of the desert-dwellers and everyone knows that it has a hump for storing water on its long treks across the desert, right? Wrong. The hump is actually a giant lump of fat, sometimes as much as 35 kilograms of it! The fat is used as fuel when then camel is running low on energy and it means that it can go for up to two weeks without eating with no problems.

The next time you complain about your vegetables tasting gross remember that it could be worse. One of the most disgusting animals around is the dung beetle – and you can guess what they eat. These tiny beetles absolutely love poo and they roll around in it all day. If they find a good bit they roll it back to their tunnels and bury it for later. If they find a great bit, they sometimes carve out a tunnel for themselves inside of it and make a new home right there. Now that's gross!

Jerboas are funny little creatures that look a bit like mini-kangaroos (very mini; their bodies are only about three inches long) with huge ears almost as big as the entire rest of their body. Their ears help them hear exceptionally well, but that isn't what makes them so special – they are unique because they never need to drink. They absorb all the moisture they need from the bits of food that they nibble on, meaning they can survive even the worst droughts without any trouble.

It's a good thing naked mole rats live in the dark because if they could see each other they wouldn't like what they saw. With their bald, wrinkly skin, long whiskers, protruding teeth and prominent snout, they have to be contenders for the ugliest animal on Earth. Fortunately, they live underground in dark burrows in the desert, and only occasionally come up to search for extra food. Like ants, they live in colonies, and we could learn a thing or two from them. They hold the record for the longest-lived rodent, able to survive for about 31 years, and are immune to many diseases, including cancer.

One of the cleverest desert-dwelling animals is the trapdoor spider. These critters build a hole in the sand and hide themselves away in it with a little roof over the top. They wait and wait until they hear something walking over the top of them and then, with a swift tug, they swing the door open and grab whatever was unlucky enough to be on the surface, which normally makes a pretty tasty treat for them.

Extreme Extinction

Although there are still millions of different animals all over the world, 99.9% of all of the different species that have ever existed are now extinct. From dinosaurs, like me, to ancient fish with armour for scales, to giant 10-foot long rodents, the Earth has been home to a huge variety of different animals that you will never get the opportunity to see. Here's a list of my 10 favourites for you:

10. Passenger pigeon: The passenger pigeon was one of the most common birds in the world during the 19th century and it travelled around in ginormous flocks containing literally billions of the pigeons. In around 1850 people started getting worried that the birds were being hunted too widely but an American committee who looked into it wisely said that 'the passenger pigeon needs no protection'. And yet less than 60 years later, in 1914, the last pigeon died in captivity, completing one of the most dramatic extinctions in human history.

9. Quagga: A quagga was an African animal that was half-zebra in the front, half-horse in the back. It looked a bit like two people had turned up to a pantomime without discussing what they were going to dress up as first. However, their ridiculous looks were no laughing matter because it made them very easy to hunt and kill, and the last wild quagga died in 1878.

8. Steller's sea cow: Georg Steller first described this massive animal in 1741 and was lucky enough to have it named after him. The sea cow wasn't so fortunate though, because by 1768 this massive animal (about 30 feet long and 10 tons in weight – only whales were bigger than the sea cow) was extinct. Unable to submerge under the water, and completely tame, this friendly sea giant made easy pickings for hungry sailors on long voyages.

7. Dinosaurs: Aaargh! My poor fellow dinosaurs! It's a lonely business being the last surviving dinosaur, which is why I keep mainly to my learnatorium and don't let people see me. After ruling the world for more than 160 million years (a lot longer than you humans have, I'd like to point out!), we dinosaurs suddenly went extinct about 65 million years ago. Human scientists aren't too sure why this was, although they suspect it was because of a giant meteor that struck the Earth. I could tell them, but it's too painful to talk about!

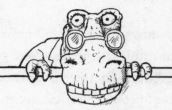

Dr Dino's Great Dying

We dinosaurs weren't the first (or the last) group of animals to suffer from mass extinction and there are way too many types of extinct animals – from huge giant millipedes to tiny mini-crabs – to possibly keep records of in my learnatorium, let alone tell you about in this book. But there is one event worth telling you about from a long time ago – 'The Great Dying'. It happened about 260 million years ago, and even I, the great Dr Dino, don't know what caused it. But I do know that it killed 96% of all species in the sea and 70% of all species on land, making it the most catastrophic time in the history of the world. Next time you get in trouble for forgetting your homework tell your teacher about it – and explain to them if they think not handing homework in is the end of the world then they need to get some perspective.

6. Sabre-tooth tiger: Now, these weren't actually tigers at all, they were really sabre-tooth cats, but that doesn't

have quite the same ring to it... These large cats were bigger than ours are today, and had one pretty scary feature – their teeth. They were about one foot long and, even though they broke quite easily, they made a very fearsome sight to anything unlucky enough to get in the way. Sable-tooth tigers became extinct about 10,000 years ago, probably because the slow-moving prey that they hunted – such as giant sloths – all died off themselves.

5. The terror bird: The terror bird was a flightless South American bird that did exactly that – it terrorised its prey. It could grow to a maximum height of three metres tall and run at speeds of about 30 miles per hour. And it had a vicious, curved beak about half a metre long! This fleet-footed predator would chase down its prey and grab them with that beak, throwing them up in the air before slamming them down on the ground to kill them. To give you an idea of how big it was, a terror bird's favourite meal was... a horse! Fortunately for humans, these non-flying terrors died off about the same time as the first people arrived in North America.

4. Megatherium: The sloths of today are cute little animals that seem sleepy at the best of times and live life at a pretty slow pace. The megatherium was an ancestor of them and was a little bit larger... six metres larger to be exact. This giant sloth wandered the Americas as recently as 8,000 years ago and, incredibly for a creature that size, it was mainly vegetarian. The human hunters that lived around them, however, were not, and the chances are this giant-sized mammal was hunted to death.

3. Woolly mammoth: In fact, woolly mammoths were only one of a number of different types of mammoths

and, weighing in at 'only' five tons, they weren't even the biggest – the Songhua River mammoths could grow to three times that size. However, they did have enormous tusks that could be 15-feet long and, as the name suggests, they were covered from head to toe in shaggy fur. Sadly, the last of these magnificent creatures died out around 4,000 years ago, killed off in part by human hunting, but mainly by climate change. One reason we know so much about them is that quite a few have been found frozen completely intact in ice, exactly as they were when they died. None have woken up when they've been thawed out... yet.

2. Megalodon: Most humans are (rightly) afraid of sharks – they can eat you alive without a second thought. But compared to the magnificent megalodon even great white sharks are truly puny. Fortunately, they went extinct about 1.5 million years ago, but these massive sharks could grow to a size of about 20 metres long, more than three times the size of the biggest sharks around today. The megalodon had seven-inch fangs and munched on giant whales, with a bite about 20 times more powerful than a lion's, making them the most powerful chomper ever to have lived on our planet. The chances are it went extinct because there simply wasn't enough food in the

ocean to keep it satisfied, and it's a good thing too, or else humans may never have dared to take to the sea.

1. Dodo: Dodos have become the most famous of the extinct animals, leading to the obvious phrase 'dead as a dodo'. They lived for thousands of years quite happily on the island of Mauritius until about the year 1598, when Dutch sailors came to the island. Within a century the bird was extinct! To be fair, it didn't help that the birds were flightless, fearless of humans, had no defences and were, by all accounts, pretty dumb. Oh yes, that as well as being big enough at around one metre high to provide a pretty large and tasty meal! (I prefer my food to be a bit bigger, but then you humans have such tiny appetites.) Still, this was the first time in the history of humankind that people started talking about the effect that they were having on the environment and the animals around them, so the dodo didn't die in vain, and now you humans are very concerned about conserving endangered animals, which is a very important job, and one that will only get harder in the future.

Dr Dino's Weirdest Animals #1

Matamata turtles are so camouflaged that you'd do well to spot them. To most people they just look like a floating log. They are masters at the art of waiting, and they can sit at the bottom of a pool for hours on end with only their reed-like nose sticking out in the air to act as a snorkel. The strangest thing about them though is the way they eat. Rather than catching and munching on fish like other turtles they simply wait for an unlucky fish to swim by, open their mouths and *suck*. The fish pops right in and the turtle can swallow it whole.

The olm is a worm-like amphibian that lives its life entirely in the dark and underwater in caves around Europe. And what a long life it leads! It can live to be up to 100 years old, but things must get quite dull: when food is scarce it can shut down its body and go up to 10 years without eating anything at all. I can normally only go a couple of hours before I start to feel peckish for a nice, big, juicy cow.

Fastest Animals

There is only one winner in a foot (or paw, or claw, or hoof, or any other type of foot you can imagine) race on land, and that is the cheetah, which can run at a top speed of 75 miles per hour in very short bursts. However, this is nowhere near the fastest animal in the world. You have to look up to see them...

1. The peregrine falcon has clocked speeds faster than any other animal, with a maximum of 242 miles per hour. It does this by climbing to an obscene height, once it spots its prey, then setting off into a dive-bomb that is very hard to escape from.

2. The spine-tailed swift definitely lives up to its name as this bird is the fastest through the air powered by its own flapping wings. It can reach speeds of up to 105 miles per hour and is so happy up in the air hunting insects that it will never settle on the ground if it can help it as it has only very short, weak legs.

3. The frigate bird can reach a very respectable speed of 95 miles per hour, helped by having the largest wings compared to its body of any bird. Incredibly, this bird can stay in the air for more than a week without coming down to the ground.

4. Hummingbirds are incredible creatures. They are tiny, measuring in at just four inches, but they live life in the fast lane. Even their hearts beat up to 1,250 times per minute, and their wings can flap around 80 times per second. The top speed one has been measured at is 61 miles per hour, which means they travel 385 times their body length every second. If a human could do that, they could polish off a marathon in about a minute and run all the way around the world in only 16 hours!

5. The cheetah also loses out to another animal in the top speed rankings. It is very difficult to measure how fast fish travel, but the black marlin has proved it is able to travel at a scintillating speed of 80 miles per hour.

Dr Dino's Did You Know?

These speeds are all impressive, but do you know which animal has travelled the fastest without the help of a machine? A human being. In 2012 a daredevil named Felix Baumgartner went to the very edge of space and jumped. Before deploying his parachute he broke the sound barrier, reaching a top speed of 843.6 miles per hour, something no other living thing has ever come close to achieving without the help of a motor.

Symbiotes

Many people think of the natural world as being unforgiving and dangerous but actually many animals work together in what are called 'symbiotic relationships' (basically the animal world's equivalent of a buddy system) to help each other out.

Dr Dino's Little Helpers

Have you eaten in the last couple of days? If so, you may not know it, but you have little helpers working inside of you. It might sound gross but millions of bacteria are always swimming around inside of your gut and without them you wouldn't be able to digest anything. In fact, without them both you and I wouldn't be able to survive at all.

Rhinos, and the other large African animals, have real problems with ticks and other small insects that leap on for a free ride and bite them for lunch too. The egret is a small bird which also gets a free ride on the back of the larger animal, but which helps them out, eating the ticks that bother the rhino so much. It's a win-win situation: the bird has easy access to fresh food and the rhino gets cleaned and taken care of. What's more, the egret is good at sensing danger and gives off a loud squawk whenever it senses a predator in the area.

Snapping shrimp love nothing more than being safe at home in their burrows at the bottom of the ocean. The problem is, whenever they come out to perform repairs on their home, search for food or even move house, they are very vulnerable to attack. Even worse, they are basically blind so not only can they not defend themselves, they can't even see what's attacking them. Enter the goby fish; this friendly chap stands guard over the top of the shrimp and flaps its tail whenever there's danger around. In return, the shrimp allows the goby to be its housemate and whenever the fish needs a rest or a place to hide it can use the shrimp's burrow.

Another couple of underwater pals are the hermit crab and the sea anemone. Much like the egret, the sea anemone hops on the back of the hermit crab as it scuttles away across the seabed. The anemone uses its tentacles to protect the crab from attackers like the octopi and in return the crab protects the anemone from hungry starfish, among other things. Another happy couple! It's a similar story with a different type of sea anemone and the clownfish. Again, they use their differing skills to protect each other from the predators searching the waters for easy pickings. These anemones deliver a powerful sting to everything that touches them, but the clownfish are covered in a special liquid that protects them.

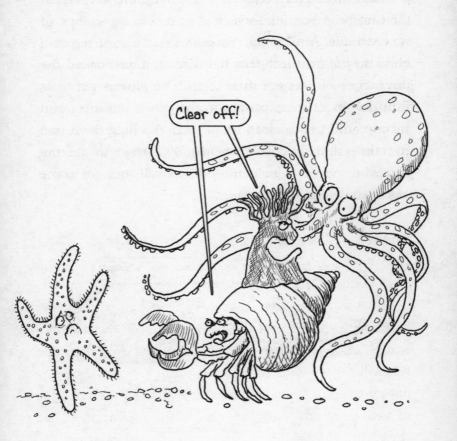

Something a T-Rex like me really struggles with is cleaning my teeth. When you have short arms and eat as much meat and bones as I do, brushing your teeth is basically impossible, which is why I'm so jealous of the crocodile. Amazingly, crocodiles stay completely still while they allow their personal dentist, a bird called the plover, to pick away at their teeth. The plovers get their fill of scraps of meat caught in the croc's gnashers and the crocodile gets a clean set of teeth, keeping them free from infection (and bad breath). I've tried to get the plovers to come to help me out as well, but for some reason they tend to fly away...

Even mortal enemies sometimes find it in their hearts to make peace at times. The woodpecker and the tree ant normally don't get on at all, and the woodpecker will try anything to get at a tree ant's nest and have a feast. However, when a woodpecker lays an egg in a tree, the two sides somehow come to an agreement. The woodpecker will leave the ants in peace, so long as the ants don't attack the egg while the woodpecker is away. I like to think of their agreement as similar to ours. Normally I wouldn't think twice about eating a couple of humans here and there – you can be quite tasty you know. But I need to pass on the knowledge of my learnatorium, and for some reason I feel that eating my students might be a bit counterproductive…

Dr Dino's Weirdest
Animals #2

The mimic octopus: this tricky
fellow is one of the greatest
chameleons in the animal
kingdom, and a mimic
as well. Not only can it
change its colour to match
its surroundings but it is
also able to twist its body
and many arms to make it
look like anything from
a sea snake to a jellyfish,
from a sting ray to a lionfish.
If there was an Oscars
of the sea world there
would be no doubt who
would win the Best
Actor prize.

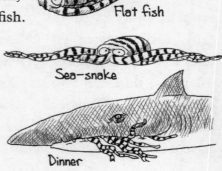

Octopus

Flat fish

Sea-snake

Dinner

The tarsier: the first thing you notice about the tarsier is its eyes. It is a tiny monkey that is the world's smallest primate, only growing four inches tall, but with individual eyes bigger than its brain. In fact, even though it's so small, it also holds the record for having the largest eyes of any mammal in the world. Unfortunately, they are too big to move in their sockets, so the tarsier is forever staring straight forward, but to compensate for that it can move its head a full 180 degrees in both directions. Its extraordinary eyes give it incredible night vision and it comes out to hunt in the dark when it can see so well that it is able to leap on a passing bird in mid-flight.

The tardigrade: the water-bear, or tardigrade, is the world's toughest animal. And it's only about 0.5mm long – too small to see without the help of a microscope. It is found almost everywhere, and is short and fat with eight legs. What's remarkable about these little critters is their ability to survive in any conditions. They can fairly easily survive any temperature between -200°C and 151°C, they can survive without water for up to 10 years, they can withstand more than 1,000 times the radiation a human can take before dying, and they can even survive in outer space for up to 10 days. They have a function that effectively lets them switch off their bodies until conditions are better for living, giving these the award for, without a doubt, the Toughest Animal on the Planet.

Raucous Rainforests

One of the most incredible habitats on Earth is the rainforest – it's my personal favourite because it reminds me of the good old prehistoric days. Even without the animals, the rainforests are a pretty special place and, even though you might not appreciate it, they are especially important to everyone on the planet because they produce so much oxygen. The Amazon rainforest produces 20% of the world's oxygen on its own!

But the really amazing fact about rainforests is that over half of ALL species on Earth, of animals and plants, can be found there. To give an example... a single pond in Brazil can contain more types of fish than all of Europe's rivers combined! And there are some pretty weird animals living there... Here are a few of my favourites:

Have you ever seen a half-giraffe, half-zebra? Well believe it or not they exist! They are called okapi and have the

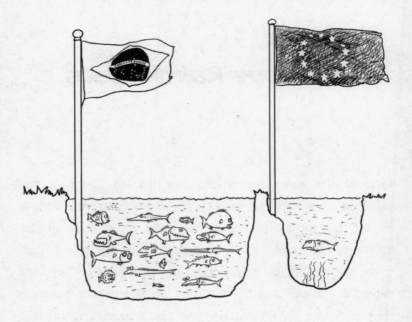

legs and marking of a zebra and the body and head of a giraffe – although with a much shorter neck. Okapis are vegetarians but eat many things we would think of as poisonous, even charcoal. And what's even more remarkable is the length of their tongues… they are so long that they can lick their ears clean, inside and out! Sadly, they are greatly endangered, and there's only thought to be around 20,000 left.

As a scientist I have a real issue with the name of a flying lemur – they can't fly and they're not lemurs. They are

more like squirrels, but with some important differences. They live almost entirely up in trees and almost never come down to ground level, but they aren't actually very good climbers. Instead, they have a flap of skin that they use like wings to glide from tree to tree. Although they are only a foot or so big, they can easily jump 70 metres from tree to tree. *Important: Don't try this at home.*

The bullet ant, or as I prefer to call it, the *paraponera clavata*, is a pretty vicious not-so-little ant. Some people call it the 24-hour ant because when it bites you it leaves you in agony for a full 24 hours. In certain tribes they use these ants in an initiation ceremony to show a boy has become a man – they fill a glove with hundreds of them and make the boy wear it. If he lasts 10 minutes then he has proved he is a man. Unfortunately, his arm is normally paralysed for a while and he will be in agony for days, if not weeks! I think I would prefer an 18th birthday party... *Important: Really don't try this at home.*

Dr Dino's Did You Know?

Did you know that every hour about 2,000 football pitches worth of rainforest are being chopped down? Because of how diverse and rare some of the plant, animal and insect species are in the rainforest, some of my fellow experts estimate that 137 species are wiped off the face of the Earth... every day. Shocking!

If you have ever been told not to wee in the swimming pool it's probably just because nobody wants to swim around in your doings. To make it clear: DON'T wee in swimming pools. But if you're in the Amazon rainforest there's a much better reason not to wee in any rivers... the candiru fish. This little eel-like fish has been reported to leap *up* the stream of wee and straight into your most sensitive area, where it releases spikes to grab hold! Some scientists think this isn't true. But nobody is volunteering for an experiment to check!

The common basilisk is a very uncommon animal. It's nicknamed the Jesus lizard because of a pretty special skill – it's only a small lizard and in the rainforest there are a lot of predators, so to help it escape it's developed the technique of running on water. Using a combination of webbing, fast feet and a light body, the basilisk is able to keep on going for around 20 metres across any water until it starts sinking. This trick only works when the lizard is sprinting though. If it tried to walk, like Jesus, it would sink just like you or me.

This is only the tip of the iceberg (although icebergs wouldn't last in a rainforest. It's too warm). There are millions of different species in the rainforests, including the glass frog, the kinkajou, the potoo and many more amazing animals you wouldn't believe if you saw them. But the rainforests are the most unexplored areas on land and there are tens of thousands of new species being discovered there every year – so who knows what you might find if you go there.

Dr Dino's Five Most Poisonous Animals

Lions, bears, sharks and even gentle T-Rexes like me all have something in common: sharp claws and teeth that can be pretty intimidating to you humans. But you forget that sometimes the most dangerous animals are the ones whose weapons you can't see. Here are five of the worst:

5. The poison dart frog is found in the rainforest and only grows to about an inch long. If you see one, don't touch it – even its skin is poisonous and contains enough poison to kill around 20 men. It's so poisonous that warring tribes in the rainforest used to dip their darts in the poison so that just a little prick would be enough to kill someone! The poison has also been developed into a painkiller which is about 200 times as good as morphine. The problem is that if you get the dose wrong by a tiny bit then the patient dies... at least they won't feel any pain ever again though!

4. Another pretty tiny, but very deadly, animal is the marbled cone snail. They can be found in the Indian Ocean, but they are quite hard to find – they are rare and only grow to about a centimetre big. If you do see one, don't pick it up! It has enough venom in a single drop of its poison to kill about 20 people. What's worse, there is no known cure, so if you touch one then it's lights out, even for a dinosaur as big as I am. Luckily, because they are so rare there have only been around 30 deaths reported over the years.

3. The most poisonous fish in the world is also found in the Indian Ocean (maybe best not to go for a paddle there!) and is called the stonefish, so named because it looks just like a stone in the sea. This is one stone you wouldn't want to step on though... It uses spines to inject venom into its victim and the sting is generally accepted to cause the worst pain known to man. It's so bad that people who are stung in the foot often ask for it to be chopped off to stop the agony! There are treatments for it, so generally the victims don't die, but if it's left untreated then it kills within a couple of hours.

Dr Dino's Dangerous Delicacy

The stonefish isn't the only deadly fish. The puffer fish is also extremely poisonous, although it doesn't ever attack humans with its poison in the sea. Instead, some humans think of it as a delicacy! (For all of my knowledge, I don't think I will ever understand you humans…) It is so dangerous to eat that only licenced chefs can prepare it in restaurants but, even so, there are many reports of deaths every year from diners in Japan who have bitten off a bit more than they can chew.

2. The most poisonous of land animals deserves its name: the king cobra. Although people think the king cobra is very aggressive, we scientists know that it actually prefers to run (or slither) away than bite. If provoked, though, it will strike and deliver quite a chomp. Even then, it often uses a 'dry bite', which means that it doesn't bother releasing any venom. If you're bitten and it does poison you, it's best to hope there's a hospital nearby – it is

poisonous enough to kill an elephant within three hours of being bitten!

1. You probably have more chance of surviving an encounter with a shark than with a box jellyfish – yet another poisonous animal found swimming in the Indian Ocean (seriously, why would anyone swim there?). They are basically transparent and so victims are normally stung before even knowing the jellyfish is there – they do after, though! The sting is very painful and can cause your heart to shut down within two minutes. Unlike most jellyfish, the box jellyfish has eyes, so they will be able to see you coming… although they have no brain, so scientists aren't sure how they know what they're seeing. That doesn't make much difference to their victims though, and there have been at least 5,567 recorded deaths because of box jellyfish since 1954.

Icky Insects

Insects have been around for a long, long time. Longer even than dinosaurs! And over that time they have evolved into many different species, so many in fact that we don't know them all. There are around one million species that have been named, but scientists think that there are around four million left to find! For example, you might think that ants all look the same, but that's just because they are so tiny you can't really tell the difference. In fact, there are about as many different species of ants as there are of birds in the world. And there are more kinds of beetles in the world then there are plants!

Honey bees are incredible insects and vital to life on Earth. Worker bees are the ones that we see flying about, and they are really hard workers. They fly around 60 miles a day, and have to make about 10 million trips to make just one pound of honey. It's a good thing they work so hard because, as they fly around, they pollinate

DO TURTLES REALLY BREATHE OUT OF THEIR BUMS?

plants everywhere they go – without them, plant-life as we know it wouldn't exist.

Found mainly in Africa, driver ants are one type of insect you don't want to get in the way of. Their colonies can contain around 20 million ants and, rather than bring food back to their anthills, they like to go on the march for it... as one big group. They form a column and just walk, attacking anything that gets in the way. It's normally pretty easy for fleet-of-foot humans to avoid them, but the marching colonies have been known to kill people when they are invalids and can't move out of the way!

Their bite is so strong that in places where stitches aren't easily available, doctors can use the ants to bite a wound together, and then rip the body off, leaving the head attached and still biting.

The best builders in the insect world have to be termites, who can build mounds up to 40 feet high, and 100 feet across. The actual nest is always below ground and the mounds are a tunnel system which can be extremely complicated. The termites themselves are only about one centimetre long, so that's the equivalent of one of you humans building something three times as high as the Burj Khalifa, the tallest building in the world.

In the 1950s, Australia started having a real problem with pollution... poo pollution. There were too many cows leaving cowpats everywhere, and it was becoming a real issue. So Dr George Bornemissza came up with a clever plan to get rid of this smelly problem: the Australian Dung Beetle Project! He introduced the dung beetle into Australia from where it lived in the

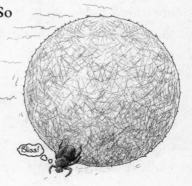

African desert and let the species have its fun with the dung. Problem solved!

Hercules was a pretty tough guy, but he's no match for the Hercules beetle, which is the strongest animal on the planet. It grows to about six inches long and can lift 850 times its weight! That's like a human lifting five double-decker buses up in the air. Fortunately, the beetle is a vegetarian and not aggressive at all, so we don't have to worry too much about it.

The most disgusting bug has to be the bot fly. This insect flies around until it finds a host, when it drops its eggs onto it. The host can be anything from a cow or a horse, to a human. The eggs hatch and the larvae (maggots) burrow into the skin where they grow… and grow… and grow. The only way to get rid of them is to cover up the breathing hole for 24 hours and then to wait for them to wriggle out – with a pair of tweezers all ready to grab them. Ewww!

Wasps probably won't be your favourite insect (with their habit of stinging humans) and they definitely won't be their dentist's, either. Wasps have a habit of sleeping while hanging by their teeth.

Dr Dino's Dangerous Insects

The giant Japanese hornet can spray acid that melts your skin. It kills around 40 people every year, making it the most dangerous animal in Japan.

Fire ants shouldn't be disturbed. If something attacks their mound they swarm and bite, causing a burning sensation (hence *fire* ants). It's hard to know how many people are killed every year, but it is almost certainly in the hundreds.

The mosquito is the most dangerous animal in the world because it carries a horrible disease: malaria. There are around 200 million cases of malaria a year, and about 1.2 million deaths. They have killed more humans than all wars combined! So next time you hear one buzzing next to you, get that fly swatter ready.

It's pretty hard to tell (for obvious reasons) but there are believed to be 10 quintillion insects on the Earth at any time. That's 10,000,000,000,000,000,000. Wow!

Super Senses

I'm constantly amazed at how rubbish human senses are. Hearing, sound, smell, touch and taste – you are bad at all of them. Most of you don't even have any common sense (like the people who swim in the Indian Ocean, or wear a glove full of bullet ants). Some animals though have absolutely super senses.

Bats might not be able to see very well, but their hearing is incredible. Some of them can even hear sounds as tiny as the footsteps of insects. The most super trick they can do is called echolocation, which means they squeak and listen to how the sound bounces back to them. From that they can tell exactly what is around them and where it all is, just as well as humans can from looking.

There is good reason for the term 'eagle eye' to mean someone who can see extremely well. Eagles can spot a rabbit in a field from a distance of two miles.

Dogs have an incredible sense of smell. When you walk you leave a miniscule scent of sweat – a dog can detect and follow this even after 24 hours, which is why sniffer dogs are used by the police. If police could train bears that would be even better – a silvertip grizzly bear can smell a dead body up to 18 miles away. But even that's nothing compared to an albatross. These large seabirds can smell fish from a mile away – even when they are in the air and the fish is underwater!

For years scientists wondered why the duck-billed platypus had such a strange-looking bill. Then they discovered something very special about it. It is packed with sensory cells that allow it to detect electricity, which means that when the platypus fishes underwater it can sense the weak electrical fields of the prey around it. (All living things generate electrical fields, which is why static electricity happens.) Other weird-looking animals, like hammerhead sharks, can do the same thing.

Some animals have the same senses as humans, but in different places. Flies, for example, have a good sense of taste, but they don't have a tongue so they taste with their legs instead, so that when they land on something they know if it's tasty enough to nibble on. Snakes, on the other hand, have a tongue but no taste buds on it. Instead it uses its forked tongue to sniff out food by its smell. Bizarre!

For many people flowers look and smell beautiful, and you might think they look that way to attract bees to pollinate them and so allow them to reproduce. This is correct... sort of. Bees don't see like humans do. They see in ultraviolet, which humans (and dinosaurs) can't see. If we could, we would realise that flowers are even more beautiful than how we see them now.

Catfish are known to be quite tasty, but would you eat a catfish's tongue? Well they don't have one... in fact their body is an entire tongue! They have around 175,000 taste buds – 20 times as many as humans do – and they can taste everything that is around them, including their prey, when water rushes over them.

Scientists have never been able to predict when an earthquake is about to strike, but animals seem to be able to. Before an earthquake occurs there are often reports of birds and bats fleeing as well as dogs howling. All sorts of reasons for this ability have been suggested, the most likely of which is their being able to sense changes in magnetic fields that occur when an earthquake is triggered, but nobody really knows.

Dr Dino's Supersense

Humans can see in what we call the visible light spectrum, quite simply because that's the spectrum of visible light we can see. But there's more light out there at different frequencies that we can't see, such as ultraviolet light and infrared light (which basically allows you to see heat). The praying mantis shrimp can see visible light, ultraviolet light and infrared light, as well as being able to see polarised light, which means it can tell which direction light is travelling in. Somehow, it takes all of this in at once, which is probably as difficult as watching four movies at once and knowing exactly what is going on in each at the same time.

In the deep darkness of underground caves, where there is basically no light, some fish have developed strange senses to help them 'see'. The blind cave fish, for example, is translucent (that's pretty see-through to you and me!)

and has an organ inside which can detect changes in the level of light, allowing it to tell if there is rock nearby so it knows where it can take shelter – and it can avoid bumping its head while swimming.

Dr Dino's Weirdest Animals #3

The dugong: closely related to the unfortunate Steller's sea cow, which went extinct in the 18th century, the dugong is an odd animal that can grow to almost four metres long and can weigh about 900 kilograms (it evolved from elephants), but is very calm and grazes peacefully on grasses that grow along the sea floor. What is bizarre about it is its mouth – it curves down into a huge hoover shape. The dugong floats along the bottom of the ocean sucking up whatever it comes across. It is thought that sailors seeing dugongs from afar might have been tricked into thinking they were mermaids. I think you'll agree they would have made pretty ugly mermaids.

The narwhal: the unicorn of the sea, the narwhal is a small whale (by small, an adult narwhal can weigh up to 1,600 kilograms, so not too small. Just small for a whale) which has a long, straight tusk coming from its head that can be up to three metres long. Scientists don't really know what it's for. Some think it is used to break the ice when the sea freezes over (narwhals are found in the very cold northern parts of the world), some think it is used in fights, some think it is a sensory organ that can smell and sense electricity, and others think it is just for show. Whatever the reason, the tusk looks very odd.

The Fitzroy River turtle: some turtles, like the Fitzroy River variety, are able to breathe in a very weird manner when submerged. Rather than having to come up for air, like most turtles, they can pump water through their cloacae (a very technical word for bum) and extract

the air from it, like fish do with gills. While very tricky, and highly amusing, even for a serious doctor such as myself, this is a disadvantage for these turtles because they require clean water and any pollution affects it quite badly. This has meant that while other turtles used to be able to breathe through their bums, the Fitzroy River turtle is the only species not already extinct, and even they are endangered. If there is one species in the world you humans must work to conserve, it is the bum-breathing turtle.

Courageous
Creatures

Over the years, animals have saved the lives of countless numbers of humans. From canaries who used to go down mines to warn people of potentially dangerous gas leaks to rescue dogs being used to sniff out survivors of natural disasters, humans have found that some animals really are man's best friends.

Todd Endris was out surfing when he was suddenly attacked by a great white shark which bit him three times, almost killing him. Incredibly, a pod of dolphins appeared and circled him, fighting the shark off and helping bring Todd to shore, where he was rushed to hospital and saved. What's remarkable is that this isn't the only time dolphins have saved humans – in fact, there have been many cases when divers or swimmers have got into trouble and kindly dolphins have appeared and pushed them to the surface, saving them from drowning.

When intruders broke into the house that Lefty, a pit bull dog, lived in, he sprang into action. Seeing one of them about to shoot his owner, Lefty leapt in front of him like a trained bodyguard and took the bullet. Sadly, Lefty lost his leg, but gained enough dog treats to last a lifetime!

If you were out hiking in the woods and came across a group of bears, what would you do? Well, Robert Biggs had other things to worry about because he hadn't just come across a family of bears, but also a vicious mountain lion! Amazingly, when the mountain lion went to attack him the bears took pity on him and chased the lion off.

During the First World War many animals served their countries, from horses and dogs to pigeons and canaries. One dog, Sergeant Stubby (that's right, he was actually promoted to Sergeant!), was particularly heroic, serving in 17 battles over two years and saving his regiment from surprise mustard attacks, finding wounded soldiers in No Man's Land and even discovering a German spy!

Sergeant Stubby was twice wounded by grenades but recovered perfectly and when he returned home to the USA he was given a true hero's welcome, even meeting the President who thanked him for his service.

Trakr was a police dog that had helped arrest hundreds of criminals and found more than $1 million in stolen cash before deservedly retiring in May 2001. However, when his handler saw the devastating attack on New York later that year – on September 11, and referred to as 9/11 ever since – he decided to come out of retirement and drove 15 hours to help in the rescue efforts. Trakr worked in devoted and valiant fashion and found the last person to be saved from the New York rubble, 26 hours after the attack. In fact, Trakr only stopped when he himself had succumbed to exhaustion and smoke inhalation, but he lived afterwards, and was considered so courageous he was even cloned, so there are more little Trakrs running around now.

Homing pigeons performed countless heroic deeds during the wars of the 20th century, carrying messages to and fro while avoiding enemy gunfire. Possibly no flight was more important than G.I. Joe's, who flew 20 miles across enemy lines to deliver a message that the village of Calvi Vecchi had been captured by the British. He arrived just as a bombing mission was about to set out which, in the belief that the village was occupied by Germans, would have otherwise killed the 1,000 British and Italian people in the vicinity. Phew!

A diving competition almost went wrong for Yang Yun, who was competing to see who could hold their breath the longest, deep underwater in a tank full of beluga whales. Her legs cramped and she was paralysed before two whales saw what was wrong and came to her rescue, lifting her up to the surface and saving her life! Despite their heroic efforts, she was disqualified...

The Sensational Seas

In my learnatorium you can find everything that humans know about the seas and oceans of the world. Unfortunately, that's not a lot... Water covers about 70% of the Earth and humans have only explored about 5% of it. Basically, there is 95% that we have no idea about! Believe it or not, we have better maps of the surface of Mars than we do of our own oceans. The reason for this is that light only travels 330 feet underwater, so beneath that everything is pitch-black. Also, the deeper you get, the higher the pressure is – at the deepest part of the ocean the pressure is 1,100 times greater than it is on the surface so sending anything to explore down there is just as difficult as sending something into space.

If you've ever choked on a gulp of the sea while swimming, it's not just salt and water you're swallowing. Each mouthful contains millions of bacteria and hundreds of thousands of tiny plankton. Don't worry though… *most* of these aren't harmful to humans.

Humans have built some pretty massive things like the Burj Khalifa or the Great Wall of China. But nothing humans have built even remotely compares to the Great Barrier Reef, a huge expanse of coral off the coast of Australia. It is millions of years old and is the largest structure that living things have built, stretching over 133,300 square miles. That's almost three times as big as England!

Whales are great communicators. Blue whales are able to make noises so high-pitched and so low-pitched that humans simply aren't able to hear them. Other whales can though, and they can detect each other from distances of up to 1,000 miles away!

One of the most intelligent animals on Earth is the dolphin (the correct order of braininess in the animal kingdom is: 1. dinosaur; 2. human; 3. dolphin!), and they can do something fairly incredible with their brains. When they sleep they only shut down half of it, so the other half can stay alert and watch out for anything trying to eat them.

Throughout the history of the sea, sailors have come back home with amazing and terrifying tales of mermaids, sea monsters and kraken (giant ship-eating squid). It's easy to think they were making it all up, but deep sea cameras have caught giant squid up to 13 metres long floating around in the darkest depths of the ocean. Very little is known about these gigantic creatures which can grow to over four times the size of an elephant, but one thing is for sure... if I were on a little wooden ship and saw one of these beasts float by, I would be pretty frightened too.

Dr Dino's Oldest Organisms

The deep sea floor is a dead place because no sunlight can reach it, so no plants and very, very few animals can survive – except that is around hydrothermal vents, where remarkable organisms live. The water comes from deep under the Earth's surface and can be as hot as 400°C. These tiny creatures can not only withstand these incredible temperatures, they actually use the heat and sulphur to create energy, so they have no need for the sun. They may well be the very oldest living animals on the planet (yes, even older than me), from which everything evolved hundreds of millions of years ago.

The greatest fishermen of the seas aren't men at all – that prize goes to the anglerfish. This is a frightening looking deep sea fish that has a long thin growth coming right out of its head that looks a bit like a fishing rod. On the end of this is a glowing 'bait' designed to look just like a tiny fish going about its business, which attracts small predators looking for an easy lunch. The problem for them is that just behind this glowing 'bait' are several rows of very sharp teeth that the anglerfish uses to excellent effect whenever anything gets in range.

Sharks are scary. Humans live in fear of them and with good reason, because they are the greatest predators in the sea. Except they aren't... if you want to see something more dangerous than a shark then go into your bathroom, look into the mirror and you will be staring at the most terrifying animal in the sea. On average, at most 10 humans are killed by sharks every year. On average humans kill 100,000,000 sharks every year. That's 10 million sharks for every one human...

Back in the good old days, when dinosaurs roamed the Earth and I hadn't even heard of humans, there were some pretty massive animals around. From giant crocodiles, giant millipedes, giant sloths... basically if you think about an animal, and then think about it bigger, that's what it used to be like. Except for one. The biggest animal to have ever lived, the blue whale, is still around.

It can grow to over 30 metres long, has a heart the size of a car and, given the chance, could fit 100 humans in its mouth.

Down in the deep depths of the sea, life can get pretty lonely and it can be very difficult for fish to find a mate. So many fish have found a way around the problem... switching genders at will. This way, whenever the two meet and take a liking to each other, they can mate straight away and become pregnant.

Dr Dino's Weirdest Animals #4

Cassowary: One of the biggest species of birds on Earth today, the cassowary is without a doubt the deadliest. Although they are quite shy, they can grow to seven feet tall and run up to 30 miles per hour (a fair bit quicker than Usain Bolt) and looks like a mix between an emu and a dinosaur.

Blobfish: there are no prizes for guessing why this fish is called the blobfish – put bluntly it looks like a big blob of slime with a huge nose and a very unhappy mouth. Although, if you were a blobfish, you would probably be unhappy too. They are consistently voted the world's ugliest animal and have even been taken on as the Ugly Animal Preservation Society's official mascot.

The Chinese soft-shelled turtle: turtles have some strange habits, and breathing out of their bums is just one of them. For years, scientists were confused about

why Chinese soft-shelled turtles would submerge their heads in puddles while standing on dry land, seeing as they breathed air, not water. Finally, it was discovered that the turtles were washing their mouths out with the water... after *weeing* out of their mouths! Somebody should really buy them a toothbrush.

Fantastic Farms

Hunting is a tradition which goes right back to the earliest animal life in the world. From the time the first tiny fish ate the first even-tinier fish, animals have been eating each other. For hundreds of millions of years we dinosaurs survived by hunting each other, and I still go out for a nibble on occasion. But humans were the first animals clever enough to raise and look after other animals to eat, and they have been farming animals for almost 15,000 years now.

You might think all farms have the same animals on them: mainly sheep, chickens, goats, pigs and cows. But around the world, humans farm all kinds of different animals from yaks and llamas to bison and water buffalo. You wouldn't want to go to a petting zoo with some of them!

Humans are pretty greedy and keeping all the people in the world fed takes a pretty large number of animals. In fact, it is believed that around 50 billion chickens are killed for food every year, which is over 100 million every day!

Dr Dino's Smelly Science

Global warming is a real issue for the future of our planet, and there's no doubt that fuel and petrol are to blame for a lot of this. But there's a much smellier problem too... cows are farting too much! There are more than one billion cows farmed around the world and each cow releases about 100 kilograms of smelly methane every year. In fact, scientists say that around 18% of all greenhouse gases released every year comes from the bums of farm animals!

Before you were born you probably annoyed your mum by giving her a few kicks in the belly to tell her you were hungry, but chickens go one further. Little chicks listen to their mother hens clucking and learn to talk while they are still inside their eggs, having whole conversations before they are even born.

Have you ever been so hot you've said you were 'sweating like a pig'? Well you actually weren't, because pigs can't sweat. Then again, pigs are definitely dirty, greedy and generally pretty disgusting aren't they? Again, you would be wrong because they are actually:

Very clean – one farmer set up a shower in the pig pen and the pigs learned to use it by themselves and loved playing in the water.

Very intelligent – pigs are the fourth most intelligent animals on Earth. They can learn tricks and have even been taught how to use joysticks to play video games.

Good eaters – although you might have been told to stop 'eating like a pig' by your parents, they actually eat slowly and prefer to savour their food.

Good athletes – adult pigs can run a mile in about six minutes.

So next time someone tells you to stop being such a pig, thank them for the compliment!

Peculiar Pets

Pets have been around for just as long as farm animals have, and it's believed that dogs and cats have always had a special place for humans. Unfortunately, I've never had a pet long enough to grow very fond of them. I have an unfortunate habit of snacking when I get hungry...

Around 15,000 years ago, humans began to domesticate wolves and they slowly became what we know as dogs, and about 12,000 years ago someone was buried with a puppy in the palm of his hand, which gives scientists like me the first real evidence of the close bond between humans and 'man's best friends'. I wonder how happy the poor puppy was with how close that bond was.

In ancient Egypt they loved dogs so much that killing a greyhound was just as bad as killing another human, and would be punished in exactly the same way. But that's nothing compared to what they thought of cats. They worshipped them as if they were demi-gods, and ranked them as far more important than humans. If there was a house fire, for example, firefighters would save the pet cats first, and then the humans afterwards!

Pets first started out as mainly *symbiotic* relationships – the humans looked after and fed the animals, and in return dogs helped with hunting, cats caught rodents, and horses could be ridden. But, as life became more comfortable for humans, they started keeping pets more for fun than anything else, and over the years people have had some weird ones...

• Pope Leo X, who lived in the 16th century, owned a white elephant called Hanno. He loved him so much that he even used to write him poems! Unfortunately, nobody in Italy knew how to look after elephants and soon Hanno became sick. The vets tried to make him eat gold as a medicine which, unsurprisingly, killed the poor elephant.

• The ancient Egyptians used to love cats, but the Pharaoh Ramses II used to love a big cat – a lion in fact. He kept one with him in his palace and named it 'slayer of my foes', which was a useful name because he used to take it into battle with him to fight by his side.

- Ivan the Terrible was a Russian ruler who was pretty terrible at keeping pets... and used them in a pretty terrible way too. He kept a number of bears in dens and would deliberately not feed them. Except for when someone angered him, and then he would throw them in with the bears!

Dr Dino's Great Cat Calamity

While cats have sometimes had the good life, like in Egypt, at other times they have been given a pretty raw deal by humans. Traditionally, witches use black cats to help them with their magic and, while you and I as scientific people know that there is no such thing as magic, other people haven't always been quite as clever. In fact, Pope Gregory IX (who was pope in the 13th century) really didn't like witches, or cats, and encouraged people to kill them whenever they could. It was a cat massacre across Europe!

Not good for cats, or for people either. Fewer cats meant more rats, and more rats meant more plague, and more plague meant more dead humans. Thanks Gregory!

One of the most famous horses of all time belonged to one of the most famous conquerors. Bucephalus was a huge horse that nobody could tame – at least, nobody until a 13-year-old Alexander the Great saw him. He soothed him and rode him, and from then on Bucephalus was his mount as he swept across the known world, conquering everything. When, finally, Bucephalus was killed in battle, Alexander was so distraught that he founded and built a city for him!

Dr Dino's Weirdest Animals #5

The honey badger: this badger actually looks nothing like other badgers, but instead more like a weasel. Unsurprisingly, their favourite food is honey, but if they can't get their paws on any of that they will eat just about anything. If they feel in the mood for a salad then they will find berries, roots and other veg to chow down on. But they often also go hunting and have been known to munch anything from snakes and lizards to turtles and birds.

What makes the honey badger so remarkable is that it is the bravest, fiercest, toughest animal in the world. Its teeth and jaw are so strong that it eats all of its prey, even bones and the shells of turtles. Its skin is so tough that even a machete can't hurt it. And it's so brave that it never backs down from a fight – honey badgers have even been known to face up to lions and fight them off!

DO TURTLES REALLY BREATHE OUT OF THEIR BUMS?

The North American wood frog: This fairly normal-looking frog doesn't seem too out of the ordinary – until winter comes around. In North America temperatures often drop well below zero, and when it does the cold-blooded frog's temperature plummets as well. So low, in fact, that the frog literally freezes and its skin becomes as hard as ice. But incredibly the frog doesn't die, even though its heart actually stops! It uses a quite disgusting trick to see it through the winter... it stores wee and sugar under its skin and uses it as an anti-freeze so that, while its body is frozen, its internal organs aren't. As long as one-third of its body stays unfrozen it is able to survive and, as soon as the temperature rises again, the frog simply thaws out, its heart starts to pump again and it hops off on its merry way.

Epic Evolution

About 3,800,000,000 years ago, one tiny organism split and became another very tiny, but slightly different, organism. Amazingly, out of that tiny bit of life, came every single animal and plant on this planet. Whatever it was, it must be feeling pretty proud of itself about now. So, in some small way, you are related to your pet goldfish, a kangaroo bouncing around Australia and even the trees of the rainforest. And yes, even to me, the great Dr Dino. Evolution is the single most incredible process on this planet, and is responsible for every living thing on it.

For something as epic as evolution is, it took a surprisingly long time for humans to accept it as fact and, indeed, some people still refuse to believe it is true. The idea of evolution had been around for a long time, and Aristotle wondered about the possibility of it 2,000 years ago, but nobody managed to truly understand the science behind it until Charles Darwin published *On the Origin of Species* in 1859, which explained natural selection and why evolution might happen. Unfortunately, many humans couldn't accept the idea that they were related to monkeys and it took a very, very long time for people to be convinced. We all know it is true though, so let's look at some of the most epic facts about it...

Do you think you could you tell the difference between the embryo of a three-week-old whale and a three-week-old human? Amazingly they look almost exactly the same, as do most other mammals at that stage. This is because you share so much of your DNA with them (because of the universal ancestor we all share) that you are much more similar than you would think – 99% of human DNA is the same as a monkey's, and 70% of it is the same as a slug's!

Dr Dino's Difficult Questions

Many tricky questions about the way human bodies work can be answered because of evolution. For example:

Q. Why do males have nipples?

A. Some parts of your body grow before your gender has been 'decided', and nipples are one of them. It is only after they are formed that an embryo's hormones mark the human as either male or female.

Q. Why do humans get goosebumps when they are cold or scared?

A. When an animal is cold it will often fluff up its hair in order to warm itself up. Thousands of years ago, humans had enough hair to do this but, recently (in evolutionary terms that is... really it is thousands of years ago) humans evolved to not be so covered in hair, because it was no longer needed (although if you look at your dad's hairy back, you might wonder if he has fully evolved or not!). Similarly, when humans had hair and were threatened, they would make their hair stand up on end, much like chimpanzees do.

Q. Why is a human's appendix not important?

A. In animals that eat grass and leaves, the appendix is incredibly important, as it allows them to digest cellulose (the tough substance that covers and protects plants). However, years and years ago humans made a good decision and took to eating meat with fruit and veg, rather than grazing on grass and leaves. The rest of the digestive system evolved but the appendix just stopped being needed, and so it does absolutely nothing at all.

Flores Island is a small place in Indonesia with a fairly small history. Around one metre small in fact. Scientists made an incredible discovery when they came across a new species of humans that had evolved and existed around 15,000 years ago – and grew to a maximum of only one metre tall. They looked exactly like hobbits, which is what the scientists call them, and they lived happily on the island hunting mini-elephants that also lived there! Sadly, the island has one thing that isn't so small... a giant volcano. At some point it erupted and wiped out all of the little people at once. Poor hobbits!

Animals have all evolved through natural selection to be the best equipped to deal with the challenges around them. Mostly these are simple things: a bird for example has developed light bones and feathers to allow it to fly, beaks for digging, pecking and carrying and talons to get a good grip on branches. Every single animal has an incredible evolutionary story to tell, but here are five quick ones for you now:

5. The peppered moth – this moth used to have a very light, almost white colouring with a few dark spots so that it could camouflage itself successfully. However, after the industrial revolution, almost every moth of this species was born with a black colouring with a few white dots. Why? Because the pollution in the air had turned all surfaces black with soot, and only the dark-coloured moths survived, so the species evolved to have a much darker colouring.

4. Crabs v mussels – in New England, Asian crabs have recently been introduced and immediately started to eat the mussels that they found there. In response to this new danger, mussels have started developing much thicker shells to foil the crafty crabs from getting at them. Pretty soon, the crabs will have to evolve to find a new technique to get to their food.

3. Elephants – these magnificent creatures are under a real threat of extinction because of poachers who kill them for the ivory of their tusks, and it is very difficult to protect every elephant. So elephants are coming up with their own form of protection... being born without tusks! Previously, only around 2% of elephants were born without them, but now it's around 10% and possibly even higher.

2. Italian wall lizards – well, actually the Croatian versions of them. In 1971, 10 Italian wall lizards were taken to a small island in Croatia. These lizards ate insects, but the island didn't have nearly enough for them to survive. So, over the next 30 years, these lizards evolved to change the way their stomachs worked and they turned vegetarian, eating plants instead of insects.

1. Pathogens – this is a group that includes nasty little things like bacteria and viruses that get inside your body and attack it, making you feel ill. Fortunately, humans have developed drugs like antibiotics to treat the diseases and kill the pathogens. Unfortunately, they are evolving to become drug-resistant. Pretty soon, all of the antibiotics won't work anymore! Fortunately, scientists know this and are working in labs around the world to develop new medicines that they won't be resistant to. They had better hurry!

Rampant
Reptiles

The most important reptiles to have ever lived are of course the dinosaurs. For millions of years, we reptiles ruled the Earth, until you mammals took over for us. There are more than 8,000 different species of reptiles in the world and we live everywhere except for Antarctica – we can't live there because we are cold-blooded, which means we get all of our heat from the sun, and we can't heat ourselves like mammals can. That's why I keep my learnatorium so toasty. You might think being cold-blooded is a big disadvantage but, because we don't have to constantly heat ourselves, we eat 40 times less food than you do for our body size.

Crocodiles are some of the most ferocious of reptiles, and they have been known to eat anything. In fact, they can sometimes be seen munching on rocks! They can't digest them, but they serve two purposes. The first is that, while a crocodile's teeth are ideal for chomping, they aren't so good for chewing, so the rocks help mash the food up in their stomachs. The second is that crocodiles are great swimmers, but they tend to float... the rocks help to weigh them down so that they can dive quickly and snap up any tasty treat they see below them.

Some snakes are extremely venomous, but actually most of them aren't at all. In fact, the majority are pretty harmless (to humans at least). In America, far more people die every year from bee stings than they do from snake bites.

The chances are that snakes had legs at one point and evolved to get rid of them so that they could sneakily slither around the ground. However, some species of snake, like the constrictor family, still show evidence of the time when they had legs and they will often have tiny leg bones with even tinier claws just visible on them.

In India you might find huge crocodile-like animals called gharials that can grow to over six metres long and have long rows of sharp teeth, which you would think you had better avoid! But there's actually no need – gharials have never been recorded as having killed a human. Although they might look ferocious, their jaws are actually very delicate, and they live by snagging small fish as they swim by, rather than going after large prey like their crocodile cousins.

Dr Dino's Reptile Family

Not all of the reptiles living on Earth died off millions of years ago with the dinosaurs. Apart from me, there were a few other survivors, and they are now the oldest animals on the planet. Turtles, for example, first appeared at least 200 million years ago, which makes them very nearly as ancient as the first dinosaurs, and they looked remarkably similar to how they do now. They, and other reptiles, are so well adapted that they have hardly needed to evolve in that entire time.

Never challenge a frog to a who-can-hold-their-breath-longer contest. You will definitely lose. They have thin, moist skin which is designed to be able to let in air. They still breathe mostly through their lungs but they are able to get a lot of their required oxygen straight through their skin!

Unlike snakes, most lizards are born with eyelids to help stop their eyes from drying out. Geckos, though, are an exception and they have had to develop a pretty disgusting way of keeping their eyes moist. Whenever they start to feel that things are getting a bit dry up there, they reach up with their long tongues and give their eyes a good lick! Gross!

They also have another weird little trick to help them survive in the wild. When a gecko is attacked it will wiggle its tail and offer it up to the predator to take a bite out of.

As soon as the attacker latches on, the gecko will drop its tail right off and scamper away as fast as possible, leaving the confused predator chewing on his tasty but rather smaller-than-hoped-for dinner.

Legend has it that chameleons can change colours completely to mimic the ground they are standing on, but this isn't really true. They don't change colours, but they can change their shade, from light to dark, depending on their surroundings. What they actually are able to do though, which is even more eye-catching, is move each eye independently of the other, so that they can look in two different directions at once!

Dr Dino's Weirdest Animals #6

The aye-aye: this primate can only be found in Madagascar, and is very weird-looking. It is nocturnal and has grey-silver fur, a little face, huge glowing red eyes and even bigger floppy, round ears. What's more, it has long spindly fingers and its middle finger is extra long and permanently extended so that it looks like the aye-aye is always giving you the finger! It is so frightening to look at that the locals believe if it points its long middle finger at you, it means you will certainly die unless you kill the aye-aye first.

Unfortunately for the aye-aye, it is actually a very shy and timid little monkey and this local belief has ended up in a lot of little aye-ayes being hunted down and slaughtered. So many, in fact, that it is now firmly on the endangered list. The long middle finger is actually used to tap on the bark of a tree up to eight times a second. The aye-aye then uses its large ears like a bat does, to listen for echoes rebounding off any larvae that might be living in the tree. Then its long finger can scoop underneath the bark and make a kebab out of any delicious bugs that might be in there.

The leafy sea-dragon: this cunning little seahorse lives off the coast of Australia and it has transparent fins and small leaf-like bits growing off it everywhere, disguising it perfectly as a bit of seaweed. This is helped as well because it is able to change colour at will. It survives by sucking up passing shrimp and tiny crustaceans that are unlucky enough to wander too close to its powerful snout. However, disguising yourself as seaweed has its disadvantages... It is very slow, and can only travel at an absolute maximum speed of 150 metres per hour. What's more, it tends to stay with big clumps of seaweed and, when there is a storm that washes all of the seaweed ashore, it also washes the helpless leafy sea-dragon to an early death on the beach, which is one big reason why these little animals are also endangered.

Arctic (and Antarctic) Animals

These animals survive living at one of the most inhospitable places on the planet. The polar opposite of living in the deserts, they need to survive biting wind, temperatures of up to -120°F and a severe lack of food anywhere, combined with far too much snow everywhere. Despite this, the poles do have a few animals that are able to make these icy lands their home, and here are a few interesting facts about a couple of them...

Polar bears

5. Polar bears can grow up to 1,000 kilograms big and can grow to more than 10 feet long. Unsurprisingly, these giant creatures don't have any predators – except for humans of course. Despite their huge size they have incredible stamina as well... they can go up to 10 days without eating and can swim for up to a week non-stop. They are able to do this because of the huge layers of fat reserves they maintain under their skin and, what's more,

that fat means that the bears never feel the cold. Actually, their big problem is not overheating when they do too much exercise!

Phew ... roll on winter.

4. The local people – known as Inuit – have hunted polar bears for thousands of years, but they also revere them, and once they've killed them the Inuit show proper respect and praise for the bear (which I'm sure the dead polar bear is extremely thankful for...). Since other humans have started moving further north and into polar bear territory, bear/human relationships have become a bit more confusing and it normally means a bad thing for the polar bear... jail. During the summer months, when food becomes really scarce, polar bears descend on the Canadian town of Churchill in their thousands trying to scavenge food. The humans try to drive them off, but if they are really troublesome then they tranquilise them and take them to a specially-made polar bear jail to serve some hard time and see out the rest of the summer!

3. Everyone knows polar bears are snow white. Except that they actually aren't. Actually, most of their fur is colourless, and the rest of it is made up of clear hollow tube-like hairs. The white that you see is really the reflection of the light off the air trapped in their fur. In zoos, polar bears will sometimes appear yellow, brown and even green. But again, this isn't their real colour. If you ever come across a polar bear wandering around and decided to shave it (something I really, really wouldn't

advise you to do if you don't want a bear whack over the head) then you will see that a polar bear's skin is actually pure black, the same colour as its nose.

2. Scientists wanted to keep track of the polar bear population, but they realised that flying over the arctic looking for a white bear on white snow was going to be pretty tricky, so they thought the easy solution was an infrared camera. But after a few trips they hadn't seen a single one! It turned out that polar bears are invisible to infrared cameras because they are so well insulated that their fur literally keeps all of their heat in.

1. In 1596 some European explorers caught a polar bear and couldn't wait to sit down to a polar feast. Everyone enjoyed the meal but afterwards they grew sleepy, irritable and then developed headaches and pains in their bones, before vomiting and their vision becoming blurry. What was worse, which they could just about see with their blurry vision, was that their skin began peeling off. For a lucky few it was just like peeling after being sunburned, but for others their entire skin came off from head to foot, leading to a coma and a pretty gruesome death!

It turned out that, while polar bear might be delicious, the liver is definitely to be avoided. It is so high in vitamin

A that just one bite is enough to send you to the hospital. So next time your parents make you eat something for the vitamin content, tell them you want to keep your skin on thank you very much!

Penguins

5. Despite spending most of their time in the water, and having flippers rather than wings, penguins are actually birds. Over millions of years their wings gradually evolved into flippers as they realised that it was a lot easier for them to fish by swimming than flying. Their distinctive colouring also came through evolution. They don't need camouflage on land because all of their predators, such as seals and walruses, are in the sea. Their dark back means anything looking down can't see them, just like their white front means anything looking up won't be able to either.

4. Penguins have no teeth, just spines in their mouth (and even on their tongues, so try not to get licked by one!) which help force the food down. Unfortunately, as they slurp the fish down, they normally swallow a whole load of sea water too. The salt isn't good for them, so they have an organ that filters the salt before they sneeze it out when they are back on land!

3. Just like crocodiles, penguins swallow little stones to help them digest their food and also to swim better. For birds they are pretty good swimmers, though. They can swim up to 22 miles per hour (much faster than a human can run) and they can hold their breath for up to five minutes. Emperor penguins are even better (well, they are emperors for a reason) and can hold their breath for at least 20 minutes and can dive as deep as 1,800 feet for food!

2. Penguins are very curious, probably because they have no land-based predators and so they are naturally pretty friendly to humans (which has worked out better for them than it did for the dodo!). Because of this, when people are around they often like to play and show off by 'tobogganing', which is when they slide across the ice on their bellies. This does help them to get around quicker, but they mainly just do it for fun.

1. One thing that you don't realise when you see penguins on TV is that they smell – very, very bad! They sometimes live in huge colonies of hundreds of thousands of penguins, and tend to produce a lot of poo, which just sits there on the ice and snow because there aren't enough flies and other insects to eat it. Some of these poo fields

are so bad that the poo stains can actually be seen from space! Hmm, maybe penguins aren't so cute after all...

Quiz

1. How fast can cheetahs run?
   A. 20 miles per hour; B. 38 miles per hour; C. 70 miles per hour; D. 140 miles per hour.
2. What does the Chinese soft-shelled turtle do with its mouth?
   A. Wees out of it; B. Uses it like a hoover to suck fish in; C. It doesn't have one; D. It sings.
3. Which insect is responsible for the most human deaths every year?
   A. The Japanese giant hornet; B. The bullet ant; C. The mosquito; D. The fire ant.
4. When did the organism live that all life is now descended from?
   A. 38,000,000 years ago; B. 380,000,000 years ago; C. 3,800,000,000 years ago; D. 38,000,000,000 years ago.
5. What do alligators do with plovers?
   A. Let them clean their teeth; B. Share their food with them; C. Eat them; D. Play games with them.
6. What was a terror bird's favourite meal?

     A. Other terror birds; B. Horses; C. Dinosaurs; D. Insects.

7. Where was the first menagerie found?

     A. Ancient Greece; B. Ancient Rome; C. Ancient China; D. Ancient Egypt.

8. What can duck-billed platypuses sense through their bills?

     A. Temperature; B. Electricity; C. Sound; D. Vibrations in water.

9. How are elephants evolving?

     A. They are growing bigger; B. They are becoming smaller; C. They are losing their tusks; D. They are losing their trunks.

10 How many sharks are killed every year by humans?

     A. 0; B. 100; C, 100,000; D, 100,000,000.

11. What is so special about jerboas?

     A. They can live for more than 150 years; B. They can hear humans walk up to 10 miles away; C. They can dig two miles under the desert to find water; D. They never need to drink.

12. What animal can breathe through their skin?

     A. Frogs; B. Crocodiles; C. Lions; D. Eagles.

13. What are a tarsier's eyes bigger than?

     A. Its own brain; B. A golf ball; C. A watermelon; D. Its heart.

14. The North American wood frog is special in what way?

    A. It can lick its own eyeballs; B. It does somersaults when it hops; C. Its heart stops when it's below freezing; D. It is the most poisonous frog in the world.

15. Why do penguins and crocodiles swallow stones?

    A. They like the taste; B. It helps them swim; C. They mistake them for eggs; D. It's part of their healthy diet.

16. What does a narwhal grow on its head?

    A. An afro; B. A helmet; C. A tusk; D. A very long moustache.

17. What colour is a polar bear's skin?

    A. White; B. Brown; C. Yellow; D. Black.

18. What was the Champawat Tigress famous for?

    A. Killing hundreds of people; B. Performing a dance at the circus; C. Rescuing a baby from a bear; D. Growing to 15 feet long.

19. How do animals contribute to global warming?

    A. They are eating too much grass; B. They are farting too much; C. There are too many of them and the world is becoming too crowded; D. Humans use too much fuel cooking them.

20. How do sniffer dogs follow someone's trail?

DO TURTLES REALLY BREATHE OUT OF THEIR BUMS?

A. They can smell the last thing you ate; B. They can smell the soap you use; C. They can see your footprints; D. They can smell the sweat you leave behind.

Answers

1.	C	8.	B	15.	B
2.	A	9.	C	16.	C
3.	C	10.	D	17.	D
4.	C	11.	D	18.	A
5.	A	12.	A	19.	B
6.	B	13.	A	20.	D
7.	D	14.	C		